In the Hospital

LEVEL 8
/ch/

Teaching Tips

Purple Level 8

This book focuses on the phoneme **/ch/**.

Before Reading

- Discuss the title. Ask readers what they think the book will be about. Have them support their answer.
- Discuss the book's focused phoneme: /ch/. Explain that it is a digraph. A digraph is two letters that combine to make one sound. /Ch/ can have three different sounds: /tch/, /sh/, or /k/. Give examples of each, such as child, chef, and ache.

Read the Book

- Encourage readers to read independently, either aloud or silently to themselves.
- Prompt readers to break down unfamiliar words into units of sound and string the sounds together to form the words. Then, ask them to look for context clues to see if they can figure out what these words mean. Discuss new vocabulary to confirm meaning.
- Urge readers to point out when the focused phonics phoneme appears in the text. Does it have a /tch/, /sh/, or /k/ sound?

After Reading

- Ask readers comprehension questions about the book. How do people who work in hospitals help us?
- Encourage readers to think of other words with the /ch/ phoneme. On a separate sheet of paper, have them write the words into columns by sound.

© 2024 Booklife Publishing
This edition is published by arrangement with Booklife Publishing.

North American adaptations © 2024 Jump!
5357 Penn Avenue South
Minneapolis, MN 55419
www.jumplibrary.com

Decodables by Jump! are published by Jump! Library.
All rights reserved. No part of this book may be reproduced in any form without written permission from the publisher.

Library of Congress Cataloging-in-Publication Data is available at www.loc.gov or upon request from the publisher.

ISBN: 979-8-88996-897-9 (hardcover)
ISBN: 979-8-88996-898-6 (paperback)
ISBN: 979-8-88996-899-3 (ebook)

Photo Credits

Images are courtesy of Shutterstock.com. With thanks to Getty Images, Thinkstock Photo and iStockphoto. Cover – LightField Studios. 3 – Tatiana Popova, Africa Studio, Paulo Ragner, grey_and, New Africa, agsaz. 4–5 – Monkey Business Images, Prostock-studio. 6–7 – SofikoS, Spiroview Inc. 8–9 – kali9, Poznyakov. 10–11 – sirtravelalot, nampix. 12–13 – Tyler Olson, wavebreakmedia. 14–15 – Dmitry Kalinovsky, Pixel-Shot. 16 – Shutterstock.

Which of these things might you find in a hospital?

Getting sick or hurt is never nice. A hospital is the place to go if medical help is needed.

If people have a problem, they may need to visit a doctor. Doctors can do a checkup to find out what is making a person sick.

If they are just a little sick or have a headache, a doctor might tell them to rest. They might tell them to go to the pharmacist for medicine to make them better.

Do not take medicine that is not for you.

In some cases, a doctor might recommend tests by experts. Hospitals have lots of technical equipment to help doctors find out about illnesses.

If someone might have a broken arm, they will need to get a scan called an X-ray. An X-ray is technology that can see inside the body to check if a bone is broken.

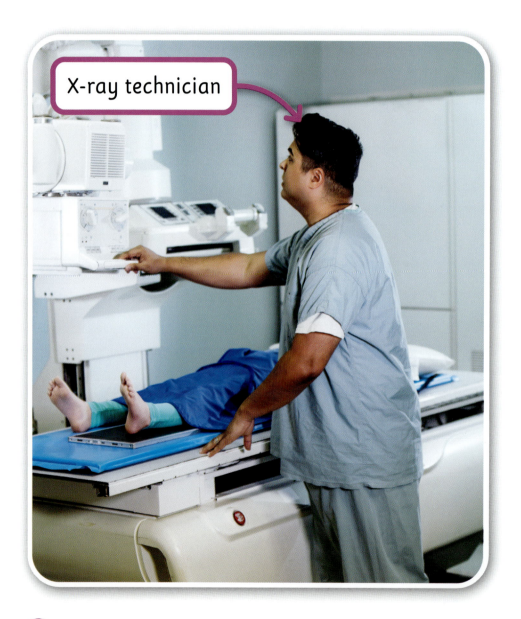

X-ray technician

If a person has a chest problem, they can see a lung expert. Their equipment can hear if the person's lungs are strong or weak.

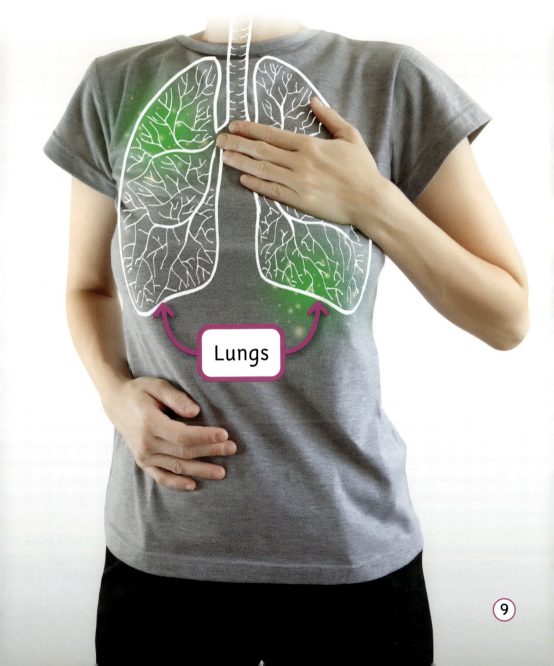

If a person has a problem with their ears, they might need to go to the hospital to get them checked. The expert will look in their ears.

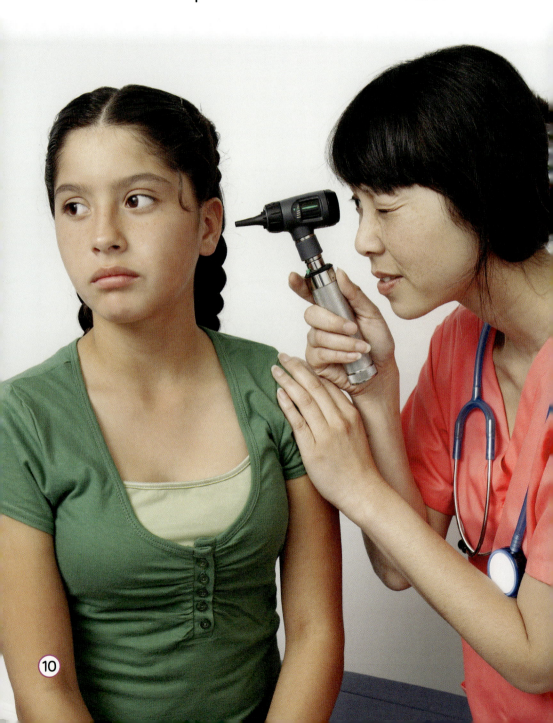

It is normal for hospitals to do a lot of tests so they can be confident that people are getting the right treatment. They may test often to keep track of any changes.

Some hospitals have branches that are just for children and babies. These branches have equipment that is the right size for kids.

Hospitals help people who are pregnant too. Nurses help people who are about to give birth. They take care of newborn babies too.

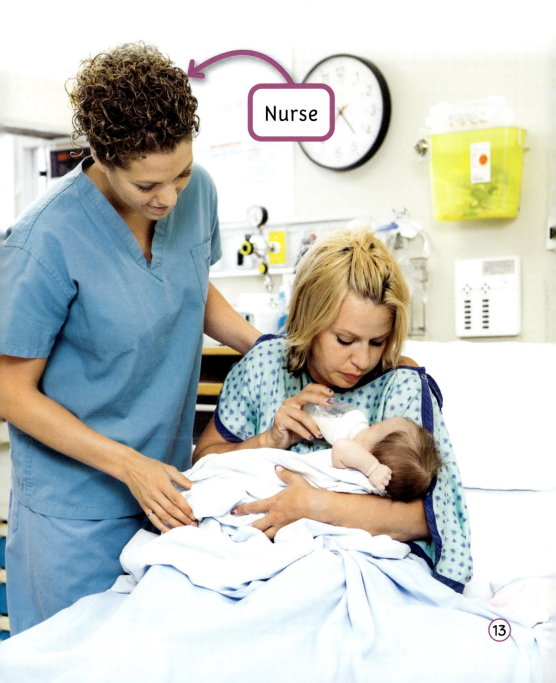

Nurse

Some hospital staff do not give treatments. They are in charge of keeping the hospital clean so that it is a safe place to be.

At the end of a shift, hospital staff change places with new staff so that there are people around to help all the time. Thanks to them, we always have people to help us when we get sick.

Say the name of each object below. Is the "ch" in each a /tch/, /sh/, or /k/ sound?

chef

cheese

school

cherry